BLOODAXE CONTEMPORARY FRENCH POETS

Throughout the twentieth century, France has been a dominant force in the development of European culture. It has made essential contributions and advances not just in literature but in all the arts, from the novel to film and philosophy; in drama (Theatre of the Absurd), art (Cubism and Surrealism) and literary theory (Structuralism and Post-Structuralism). These very different art forms and intellectual modes find a dynamic meeting-point in post-war French poetry.

Some French poets are absorbed by the latest developments in philosophy or psychoanalysis. Others explore relations between poetry and painting, between the written word and the visual image. There are some whose poetry is rooted in Catholicism, and others who have remained faithful to Surrealism, and whose poetry is bound to a life of action or political commitment.

Because it shows contemporary French poetry in a broader context, this new series will appeal both to poetry readers and to anyone with an interest in French culture and intellectual life. The books themselves also provide an imaginative and exciting approach to French poets which makes them ideal study texts for schools, colleges and universities.

Each volume is a single, unabridged collection of poems presented in a parallel-text format, with the French text facing an English verse translation by a distinguished expert or poet-translator. The editor of each book is an authority on the particular writer, and in each case the editor's introduction presents not only a critical appreciation of the work and its place in the author's output but also a comprehensive account of its social, intellectual and cultural background.

The series itself has been planned in such a way that the individual volumes will build up into a stimulating and informative introduction to contemporary French poetry, giving readers both an intimate experience of how French poets think and write, and a working overview of what makes poetry important in France.

T0166074

BLOODAXE CONTEMPORARY FRENCH POETS

Series Editors: Timothy Mathews & Michael Worton

Timothy Mathews is Professor of French at University College London. His books include *Reading Apollinaire: Theories of Poetic Language* (Manchester University Press, 1987 & 1990) and *Literature, Art and the Pursuit of Decay in 20th Century France* (CUP, 2000). He co-edited *Tradition, Translation, Trauma: The Classic and the Modern* (OUP, 2011) with Jan Parker, and co-translated Luce Irigaray's *Prières quotidiennes/Everyday Prayers* (Larose/University of Nottingham Press, 2004) with Irigaray. The first volume in this series, *On the Motion and Immobility of Douve* by Yves Bonnefoy, has an introduction by him.

Michael Worton was Vice-Provost and Fielden Professor of French Language and Literature at University College London. He has published extensively on contemporary French writers, with two books on Michel Tournier, and co-edited *Intertextuality* (1990), *Textuality and Sexuality* (1993), *Women's Writing in Contemporary France* (2003), *National Healths: Gender, Sexuality and Health in a Cross-Cultural Context* (2004), *Liberating Learning* (2010) and *French Studies in and for the 21st Century* (2011). The second volume in the Bloodaxe Contemporary French Poets series, *The Dawn Breakers* by René Char, is introduced and translated by him.

For further details of the Bloodaxe Contemporary French Poets series, please see pages 7 and 149 of this book.

BLOODAXE CONTEMPORARY FRENCH POETS: 9

GUILLEVIC

Carnac

Translated by
JOHN MONTAGUE

Introduction by
STEPHEN ROMER

BLOODAXE BOOKS

BLOODAXE CONTEMPORARY FRENCH POETS: 9
Guillevic: *Carnac*

Original French text of *Carnac*
by Guillevic © Éditions Gallimard 1961.
English translation © John Montague 1999.
Introduction © Stephen Romer 1999.

ISBN: 978 1 85224 393 7

First published in 1999 by
Bloodaxe Books Ltd,
Eastburn,
South Park,
Hexham,
Northumberland NE46 1BS.

www.bloodaxebooks.com
For further information about Bloodaxe titles
please visit our website and join our mailing list
or write to the above address for a catalogue.

Supported by
**ARTS COUNCIL
ENGLAND**

This book is supported by the French Ministry
for Foreign Affairs, as part of the Burgess Programme
headed for the French Embassy in London by
the Institut Français du Royaume-Uni.

This is a digital reprint of the Bloodaxe 1999 edition.

CONTENTS

GENERAL EDITORS' PREFACE

The Bloodaxe Contemporary French Poets series aims to bring a broad range of post-war French poetry to as wide an English-speaking readership as possible, and it has specific features which are designed to further this aim.

First of all, each volume is devoted to a complete, unabridged work by a poet. This is designed to maintain the coherence of what a poet is trying to achieve in publishing a book of poems. We hope that in this way, the particular sense of a poet working within language will be highlighted. Secondly, each work appears in parallel translation. Finally, each work is prefaced by a substantial essay which gives a critical appreciation of the book of poetry, of its place in its author's work, as well as an account of its social and intellectual context.

In each case, this essay is written by an established critic with a love of French poetry. It aims not only to be informative, but also to respond in a lively and distinctive way to the pleasures and challenges of reading each poet. Similarly, the translators, often poets in their own right, adopt a range of different approaches, and in every case they seek out an English that gives voice to the uniqueness of the French poems. The quality of the translations in the series has been widely recognised: two of the titles are Poetry Book Society Recommended Translations, an award given to only four books a year translated from any language.

Each translation in the series is not just faithful to the original, but aims to recreate the poet's voice or its nearest equivalent in another language: each is a translation from French poetry into English poetry. Each essay seeks to make its own statement about how and why we read poetry and think poetry. The work of each poet dovetails with others in the series to produce a living illustration of the importance of poetry in contemporary French culture.

TIMOTHY MATHEWS
MICHAEL WORTON
University College London

INTRODUCTION

Eugène Alphonse Marie Guillevic was born at Carnac, in the Morbihan peninsula of Southern Brittany in 1907. By the time he published his first full collection *Terraqué*, in 1945, he had jettisoned his Christian names – too reminiscent of a difficult childhood and a harsh mother – and wrote under the rugged single name of Guillevic. He was born into a working-class family descended on both sides from peasant stock, agricultural labourers and village artisans. His father was at first a sailor, and then joined the *Gendarmerie* shortly before Eugène was born; his mother was a seamstress. In all of its aspects, the indelible imprint of Guillevic's Breton childhood is crucial to his poetry: as his friend Jean Tortel has written of the author of *Terraqué* and *Carnac*: 'no poetry starts out from so close to the lived as his'. By way of introduction to this poet, and in particular to his collection *Carnac*, it is indispensable, therefore, to evoke that childhood in some detail.

Carnac: early years

In his book of interviews, *Vivre en poésie / Living in Poetry* (1980), Guillevic provides a lively, anecdotal background to the 'secret work' of the poet, and I acknowledge it here as the major source of what follows.

He was born into a largely Breton-speaking community, although French was compulsory at school (Breton was forbidden, along with spitting on the floor), and Guillevic never learned more than a few expressions in Breton, picked up from his parents, who spoke the language when they didn't want their two sons to understand. In 1907, Brittany was still a relatively backward province of France, overwhelmingly dependent on fishing and agriculture. Guillevic's grandfather's family, for example, all lived in a single room, along with the cow. It was also a community sunk in Catholic traditions, with all that entails of superstition, old wives' tales and ritual. As a boy, he was taken by his mother to the famous 'Pardons', of the kind unforgettably described by Tristan Corbière (one of Guillevic's heroes) in his poem on the Pardon at Sainte-Anne-la-Palud, or painted by Paul Gauguin. Guillevic recalls his mother, a religious 'bigot' (his father was non-practising) taking him to Pardons at which he walked on his knees and drank water into which the stumps of beggars had been plunged. It is not surprising then, given the maternal pressures, that Guillevic started out as an anxious Catholic, obsessed by guilt and sin. His later devotion to dialectical materialism and to the Communist Party must in part be understood as a reaction against his earliest impressions. As he records it in *Vivre en Poésie*, his first memory (by this time he was at Jeumont, on the Belgian border) was of 'a memory of guilt, in a police station, under a tyrannical mother'.

Fear, indeed, seems to have been the ubiquitous emotion: of an untender mother, of a bullying schoolmaster, of childish nightmares, elemental in quality (the image of ogre-like menhirs on the move finds it way into *Terraqué*), of his contemporaries at school where he was 'the poor boy', and, worse, the son of the local policeman, subject to the scorn of the sons of the *petite bourgeoisie*. Luckily for Guillevic, he was strongly built (both his father and uncle were physically colossal, the undisputed *hommes forts* of the region, even though the latter was actually stoned to death for 'going with' a prostitute...). In any case, the young poet soon learned the use of his fists to earn respect. As he writes in an important, inaugural poem 'Garçon':

> Mieux valait se faire des bâtons avec le houx
> Pour la gueule des chiens,
> Mieux valait se battre dans les genêts,
> Rendre coup pour coup et deux coups pour un –
>
> It was better to cut holly sticks
> To use against the dogs,
> Better to fight in the broom,
> Blow for blow, and two blows for one –

This poem is an early delineation of the tension, present in so much of Guillevic's work, between the necessity for toughness and self-sufficiency, for a rocklike independence, and the yearning for maternal tenderness and for the self-forgetfulness of erotic love. We shall find these themes developed and consciously mythologised in the sequence of poems that make up *Carnac*, discussed below.

In his years at Saint-Jean-Brévelay, a small town near Carnac to which his father was posted from 1912 to 1919, Guillevic was part of a gang of boys that went fishing, bird-nesting and stealing from orchards, of the kind familiar from a thousand such country reminiscences. But it was also here, and fishing by the sea, that he became familiar with a vast elemental solitude and with those impulses of pantheistic enthusiasm so recognisable to us as the staple of Romanticism. The traces of this early, secret communion are everywhere present in the work of the mature poet. As Guillevic says of Saint-Jean-Brévelay: 'It wasn't visual for me, so much as sensual. The feel of that earth was my real schooling.'

But there was little time, and still less encouragement, for these solitary ecstasies. From an early age the necessity of 'standing on his own two feet', of 'paying his way', of 'cutting his coat according to his cloth' – the clichés here are of the essence – was impressed upon Eugène. 'What counts for me is primary school. I have the feeling I never learned anything after that. What I know of history and geography...comes from primary school. It marks and penetrates one.' Like his younger *confrère*, Yves Bonnefoy, who was born into similarly modest circumstances, Guillevic owes much to Jules Ferry, the great pioneer of civic education in France: it was Ferry who, towards the end of the 19th century introduced all the salient features of French national education – free – and obligatory – primary schooling for all, secular or *laïque* in nature.

At school, Guillevic showed some inclination for mathematics, especially geometry, which he was later to put to use in his collection of poems, inspired by geometrical figures, *Euclidiennes* (1967). In 1919, Guillevic's father was transferred to Ferrette, a town in Alsace, hilly country near the Swiss border. He completed his education at the Collège d'Altkirch, which involved four hours' travel by train every day. It was on the train that he read voraciously – La Fontaine, Hugo, Lamartine, Jean-Jacques Rousseau, and then Baudelaire, Verlaine, Rimbaud; but also German poets like Mörike, and later Trakl, whose work became an abiding passion and which he was to translate.

'Les mots,/ C'est pour savoir...' / 'Words/ Are for knowing...'

Guillevic the Breton poet: the primitive, the elemental, the menhir-like and monolithic. Clusters of adjectives like these have come to overlay his name, like geological accretions. But it should be made clear that Guillevic is by no means a Breton *bretonnant*, he has shown no interest in learning, let alone writing in, that language. His passion is for the French language, and his lexical curiosity for French, as an *acquired language*, is celebrated. He has put on record his devotion to dictionaries. The word *terraqué*, to take a famous instance, which means a marshy estuary between land and sea, was unknown to many of his literary associates. His abiding respect for French, as the language of authority and of the élite (and this, despite his militant egalitarianism in the social and political context) is remarkable, and it is accompanied by what Tortel calls, in an apt phrase, a particular 'violent timidity', with which he approaches words: 'Les mots/ C'est pour savoir' as he puts it definitively in *Terraqué*.

In Guillevic's mind, this respect for French combined with his notion of another language, that of the poem. There is an almost Mallarméan exigency in Guillevic's insistence that ordinary language is like string ('la ficelle'), while the language of poetry should be tense and solid and unbreakable, like wire ('le fil de fer'). Or like stone. For a poet whose natural tendency is towards a certain facility, the scrupulous restraint Guillevic imposes upon his compositions, his quest for the lapidary is especially noteworthy. The characteristic density and elliptical form of his poetry, its 'scrupulous meanness', to echo Joyce, seems to have been dictated to him, curiously enough, in a recurring dream, in which he carved lapidary phrases on the beech trunks around Ferrette.

A Communist at the tax office

Scrupulousness, weighing and measuring, calculating exact amounts, became part and parcel of Guillevic's professional life, when he joined the government tax office in 1926, and worked for what was then considered a 'noble administration', under the impressive figure of the local 'receveur de l'Enregistrement', or fiscal registrar. For the next thirty years or so, Guillevic earned his living as a diligent government employee, a veritable wage-slave, in the tax office; from 1936 he held an important post in the Ministry of Finance itself, in Paris.

It is no accident that his reading of Marx, and adhesion to the French Communist Party (in 1942) coincided not only with the Occupation, but with his professional "elevation". There can be few *métiers* that entail such an almost brutal confrontation with the "real", and its hardships, than the office of the fiscal registrar, which involves making detailed inventories, and evaluations of land, property and movable possessions. The austere and mysterious encounter with the otherness of objects, like the celebrated 'armoire' which opens Guillevic's first collection *Terraqué*, inaugurating a series of poems simply called 'Choses' ('Things'), is not entirely alien to the cold eye of the tax-assessor. Critics have all noted Guillevic's fascination, even fear, of the 'alterity' of objects, and of his apparent need to 'rescue them' from their benightedness. Writing in *L'Entretien des muses* about Guillevic's attitude in 'Choses', Philippe Jaccottet comments: 'What matters for him is to *confront* that secret, that dark and hidden power: either to exorcise the threat it poses, or to bring its promise to fruition...' There is this remarkable *obstinacy* in Guillevic, this refusal, as it were, to turn away from the brick wall, until it *gives*: We shall see it in *Carnac*, where he tries, patiently and at length, to 'fathom' the sea.

Paris and 'la crise des *Sonnets*'

By the time of *Terraqué*, published by Gallimard in 1945 (though poems from it were published earlier, in the *NRF*, which was edited by Drieu la Rochelle at the time, with whom Guillevic had a curious love-hate relationship), the ungainly Breton youth was now a mature, respected figure on the Parisian poetic scene. He attended weekly meetings at the 'Pont Mirabeau', where a group of poets including Jean Tortel, Maurice Fombeure, René Massat and others met for discussion. But it was Jean Follain who introduced Guillevic to this circle and who was one of the first to recognise the Breton poet's original contribution, as the poet 'who gives refuge to the frightened creatures (and things)'. In fact, there is a similar minute attention to humble objects, and their tragic resonances, in Follain's own work (he was brought up in the countryside of Normandy). Less fruitful, in many ways, were Guillevic's relationship with the Surrealists. While he admired their revolutionary politics, he was less at ease with their literary mannerisms or aesthetic. Indeed, it is difficult to imagine how Guillevic, with his hard-won sense of life's realities, could ever countenance the importance given by Breton and his colleagues to dreams, and 'automatic' compositions. For him, Surrealism was alien in another sense as well, being a quintessentially urban movement.

Before considering the *Carnac* sequence in more depth, which is the primary function of this introduction, a brief word needs to be said about what has become known as 'la crise des *Sonnets*' ('the crisis of the *Sonnets*') in Guillevic's career. The sonnets referred to are the *Trente-et-un sonnets* (*Thirty-one Sonnets*), published in 1954 with a preface by Louis Aragon. As poems written explicitly to further the Communist cause, and defiantly addressed to the 'Hommes de plus tard' ('Men of the Future'), they represent, as Guillevic later came to see all too clearly, a serious aberration. Aragon, in a

13

disingenuous preface, hailed Guillevic's return to regular metre as an (egalitarian and patriotic) return to a 'national poetry' – whatever that might be. In the days immediately after the war, Guillevic was convinced of the need for militant action, and that must come before his calling as a poet. He had consciously adopted, as he later admitted, the Communist *langue de bois* (political cant). Khrushchev's anti-Stalin speech at the 20th Party Congress in 1956 came as much as a shock to Guillevic as to nearly all his fellow-travellers. And although he remained a member of the PCF until 1980, it is safe to say he was increasingly a less orthodox, less hard-line, more eccentric one as time went by.

Carnac

Guillevic began writing *Carnac* at the very end of the 50s. It coincided with his early retirement from the slavery of the tax office, and with an extraordinary renewal, for a poet now 52, of the concentrated power that had produced *Terraqué*, nearly 20 years earlier. Guillevic expresses it thus: '*Carnac* was a great joy for me, a deliverance. I recovered myself, my country, the earth and the sea; I relived everything that I had been'. After *Carnac*, Guillevic went on publishing collections with astonishing regularity right up to his death in 1997. But I suspect the high points of his art are contained in this collection, and in *Terraqué*. In what remains of this introduction, I will examine the *Carnac* sequence in more detail.

On the edge of the void

On the poet's own authority, the sequence was triggered by reading an essay by Gaétan Picon on Mallarmé, in which the critic writes of 'the drop of nothingness [*néant*] which the sea lacks'. It is indeed the rich semantic charge with which Mallarmé invests the word 'néant' that helps us apprehend the metaphysics underlying Guillevic's poem. (In case anyone should find 'over-intellectualised' what follows, it is worth reflecting on what Michael Hamburger, in *The Truth of Poetry*, once wrote about Yves Bonnefoy's poetry, 'that it assumes an order of pure ideas...' And while Guillevic is less of a theorist than Bonnefoy, his poem – knowingly – *does* take issue with such things as Mallarméan poetics and the realm of 'pure ideas'; and if we ignore this, we will miss much of the meaning.)

In the implications of Mallarmé's poem 'Un Coup de dés' ('A Throw of the Dice'), and in the moving notes made after the death of his son Anatole, one of which contains the bewitching phrase 'vent de *rien / qui souffle /* (là, le néant / ? moderne)' ('wind of *nothingness / that blows /* (that is, the nothingness / ? of the modern)'), we find perhaps the germ of what has been called the 'negative theology' common to so many French poets of the modern and contemporary era. The key philosopher here is probably Heidegger, in particular his notion of the absence of God, experienced both negatively and positively. In the 'Post-scriptum' to his essay entitled *Das Ding* (The Thing), Heidegger explains that 'the default of God and the divinities is absence. But absence is not nothing; rather it is precisely the presence, which must first be appropriated, of the hidden fullness and wealth of what has been and what, thus gathered, is presencing, of the divine in the world of the Greeks, in prophetic Judaism, in the preaching of Jesus.'

Guillevic has his *sacré*; and like Yves Bonnefoy, in many ways he is a 'mystic without a God', his *sacré* is the unmediated, non-conceptual apprehension of Presence (in the Heideggerian sense also), which founds the enterprise of poetry and its language. But Guillevic's epiphanies are rarely made explicit, and certainly not 'interpreted' as such, which is why care must be taken in employing a term like 'presence'.

Nevertheless, *Carnac* might be described as a remarkable attempt to found a new pagan religion: sea-worship. It is wholly appropriate to the place and to the man – 'un homme de la préhistoire' ('a man from prehistory') – as Guillevic often referred to himself. Built like a menhir – the comparison is unavoidable – he feels a mysterious affinity with the men ('Those of the menhirs') who aligned those massive stones, menhirs, dolmens, cromlechs, sacrificial altars, if such they were. Perhaps they raised them in homage to the elements, but they also raised them to give weight and dignity to themselves, in the face of brute force. And Guillevic's sea-worship has precisely this double aspect, composed as it is of homage and rivalry. Certainly his is a robust, argumentative, often witty Old Testament type of address to the 'divine': Guillevic apostrophises the sea, taunting, flattering, pleading, sympathising, even tempting it by turns. At one point he calls, mischievously, for a kind of 'pax':

Allez donc! Allez!	Go on then! Go!
Trêve de nos pointes.	A truce on our headlands.
Paix sur toi, la grande,	Peace to you, great one,
Et paix sur nous.	And peace to us.

But the contest is, in the end, fruitless, and so is the homage, as the bleak final couplets acknowledge:

Toi, ce creux	You, that trough –
Et définitif.	Definitive.
Moi qui rêvais	I who dreamt
De faire équilibre.	Of achieving balance.

As if there were nothing for it in the end, but to turn his back on the sea, or ignore it, and strike inland. It should understand, he says earlier, 'Que l'on peut préférer /Y vivre loin de toi' ('That one can prefer / To live far from you').

To return to the theme of that inaugural 'néant' I touched on earlier, Guillevic evokes the God-in-His-Absence, so to speak, explicitly:

Tu es pour quelque chose
Dans la notion de Dieu,

Eau qui n'es plus de l'eau,
Puissance dépourvue de mains et d'instruments,

Pesanteur sans emploi
Pour le temps qui n'est pas.

You represent something
In the notion of God

Water no longer water,
Power deprived of hands, instruments

Weight without function
For which time doesn't exist.

Behind this 'néant' lurks also, of course, the formless void of Genesis, where 'darkness was upon the face of the deep'; and Guillevic conjures the drama of the 'fiat lux' in his poem – especially the way the knowledge of the void lingers, and pierces the multiplicity of created forms. Like the God of Genesis also, the sea desires attributes, manifestations, light: we find the sea as it were 'courting' the rocks to provide itself with a 'skeleton' – 'Go on, go on,' urges the poet, 'Flatte-les de tes vagues // Et reste invertébrée' ('Caress them with your waves // And remain invertebrate'). But what the sea does produce, either deliberately or through negligence, and this is part of its profoundly equivocal nature in the poem, are the monsters of the deep, 'Those monsters who penetrate / The place of our nightmares.'

The 'timid things' that finally did emerge from the sea on to the land, are imagined as 'abandoning' the sea – hence its obscure resentment. For Guillevic, as much as for Eliot, the living sea is both 'menace and caress'; its nature is alternately maternal and monstrous, appeased and vengeful. But these 'attributes' are after all only fanciful, provided by the poet who pushes anthropomorphism to the limit; and Guillevic recognises this; the sea is finally the Absent, the Other, the Unknowable – 'le creux', or the Hollow, to use his own word. Even worse: the sea is indifferent.

Clearly, the stakes in this poem are high: despite the flashes of sly humour, it is, as Guillevic affirmed in an interview shortly before his death, 'un poème de passion'. From *Terraqué* onwards, Guillevic is haunted by the *alterity* of the world and its objects, their seeming self-sufficiency. In his remarkable, pioneering essay on Guillevic, Jean-Pierre Richard places this *hantise*, or obsession, with alterity at the heart of the work: 'As violent in its impact as obstinate in its withdrawal, the world is fundamentally outside of us.' And further: 'From the object the only lesson we can learn, no doubt, is that of knowing there is nothing to learn...' This 'refusal' of the object provokes in the poet, especially in his early work, an almost frenzied attempt to enter it; in one poem ('Exécutoire') we find him literally beating his hands and head against a wall:

Voir le dedans des murs	To see the inside of walls
Ne nous est pas donné.	Is not granted us.
On a beau casser	Break them as we might
Leur façade est montrée.	They remain façade.

As we have seen, the fundamental alterity of the sea is the inaugural premiss of *Carnac*; and it is this unbridgeable gulf between perceiving subject and the object of perception that provides its dynamic, in the sense that there is a void to be filled. In terms of language, it is the non-coincidence of sign with signified that haunts the poet (or a poet of Guillevic's stripe), and his passion is to persuade himself (and his reader) on the contrary of their coincidence. This dilemma is dramatised explicitly in the following section. Wherever the perceiver is, whatever one's angle of vision, one is always 'at the doorway':

À la porte de l'océan	At the ocean's door
Et parlant, parlant.	And speaking, speaking.
Le difficile,	The difficult thing
C'est d'être lui	Is to be the ocean
Et si tu l'étais	And if you were
C'est de rester toi,	To remain yourself,
Assez pour savoir	Enough to know
Que tu es les deux	That you are both
Et pour en crier.	And to shout it out.

The poet, that is, must straddle the two existences at once, if he is to speak. Total fusion with the object would silence him, much as the mystic is silenced at moments of self-oblivion in communion with God, though he can, it is true, 'come down', and recount his vision retrospectively.

It remains for us to examine more systematically the strategies deployed by Guillevic within the context of this non-identification; what can he, metaphorically, "throw at the sea" to elicit a response, to re-establish some balance, to make contact? Throughout the sequence, a series of themes, or approaches, is worked out; some of them occur just once, others recur, rather in the manner of musical leitmotifs. There is the appeal to the feminine, in its widest application – to the tender and the maternal – prompting in the subject a longing for a primal bliss or oblivion; there is, concomitantly, the appeal to the "masculine", to the harsh dignity of the prehistoric menhirs, set up, as it were, in vertical opposition to the sea's morale-sapping horizontal. There is the pathetic appeal to the memory of a dead sweetheart, who might tame the sea as in some primal mythological scene; there are the mediating forces of wind and rain that nuance the principal dialectical "war" between the sun and the sea. There is the poet's appreciation of the sea as a kind of muse, whom he "baptises" with the flowers and spices of the earth; there is his wilful turning away, like a lover trying to make his beloved jealous. And so on. All these themes have to be understood within the all-enclosing dialectic between, essentially, being and non-being, the lineaments of which I have already sketched.

'La Mère' / 'The Mother'

The appeal to the feminine, in particular to the maternal, is a key aspect of Guillevic's poetry, especially present in *Terraqué* and *Carnac*. Against it must be set the "masculine" precepts of independence, endurance, self-sufficiency, harshness. In *Carnac* this dialectic takes on an epic quality in the "war" between the sun and the sea, between the Apollonian and the Dionysiac, the masculine and the feminine, the conscious and the unconscious, sanity and madness, the 'symbolique' and the 'imaginaire' to adopt Lacanian terminology, even – given Guillevic's politics – a kind of Hegelian dialectic between history and nature, evolution and identity. As I have mentioned, one salient feature of Guillevic's psychological make-up comes from a harsh, unloving mother – hence the longing for affection and, conversely, the extreme mistrust of the 'maternal' occasioned by its being witheld, or even betrayed. It is certainly one of the richest veins in his work, and often very poignant in that these 'elemental' wars contain a covert autobiography of the poet. The psychological necessity for differentiation, for independence, against the 'viscous', or the 'mucus' of the feminine (the words are Guillevic's) find memorable expression in his poem 'Garçon' ('Boy'), from *Terraqué*:

Mieux valait faire la petite guerre dans les champs
Que s'angoisser au soleil couchant,
À cause de son sourire peut-être, à elle,
Ou à cause de tout.

It was better to wage petty warfare in the fields
Than to brood on the setting sun,
Because of her smile perhaps, hers,
Or because of everything.

In 'Ensemble', again from *Terraqué*, the sea is evoked in boldly sexual terms:

Et l'homme peut le soir retrouver dans un lit
Le goût frais de la mer
Entre des cuisses ouvertes.

At evening the man can find in his bed
The fresh taste of the sea
Between opened thighs.

In *Carnac*, the sea manifests the dark, even terrifying aspect of the maternal, as a womb in which nightmarish monsters multiply and grow. This obsession eclipses any joyous idea of sexual desire, though that is present too:

On ne peut pas te boire,   One cannot drink you,
Tu refuses nos corps.   You refuse our bodies.

Mais on te touche   But one can touch you
Un peu.   A little.

And it appears, at times, gentle and caressing, and that, too, is perhaps true, though the poet's mistrust is strongly implied.

In the sun-sea dialectic, Guillevic plays knowingly, perhaps almost too knowingly at times, with the philosophical and psychological oppositions that lie ready to hand. But the subversive aspect of the sea, its undifferentiation, its unsignified mass, is well caught:

Sans toi d'ailleurs, soleil,   Without you, indeed, sun,
La mer serait encore   The sea would still be
Cognant à l'infini,   Striking at the infinite,
Mais alors dans ce noir   But in this dark, then

Qu'on suspecte la mer	Let's suspect the sea
De vouloir devenir	Of wishing to become
Quand tu es là,	When you are there,
Soleil.	Sun.

The desire for oblivion, for the return to that formless void, and the menace that poses to individuation, to being itself, scarcely needs pointing out.

'Ceux des Menhirs': Prehistory

The second main theme or leitmotif in the poem turns around 'ceux des menhirs', the prehistoric men who raised those stones in their strange alignments, and who lived in what Guillevic simply calls 'le sacré' – a term we need to inspect more closely. On many occasions, and not entirely in jest, Guillevic described himself as a 'man from prehistory'. As he explained in *Vivre en poésie*: 'I live more with the elements than in society. Hence my uneasiness with psychology and analysing human relationships.' He means by this, essentially, the quasi-mystic sensation of total integration of his consciousness with the monolithic presences of rocks, the sea, the wrack, and the gulls: a monumental solitude, as well. He felt this fishing in Brittany, off the Île de Groix, where there are steep cliffs, as opposed to the beaches of Carnac.

It is not difficult to imagine, in such a context, being invaded by an Olympian sense of power, something expressed by Nietzsche when he wrote 'How could there be a god other than myself?' The German philosopher undoubtedly stirred the young poet, and he glosses Nietzsche's question with a startling simplicity: 'I believe that all poets cast themselves as God.' And we come close to his notion of 'le sacré' when he declares: 'At the root of all religions is a great poetic text. There is no sacredness without poetry, and no poetry without sacredness.' And he adapts Mallarmé's phrase, originally applied to music: 'By means of poetry, we must reclaim our own from religion, or everything man has invested in it of himself and his capacities.'

Now Carnac, with its menhirs, and, in all probability (it is Guillevic's own belief) its altars for animal or human sacrifice, was, and remains (despite the holiday "villas" of the resort), a sacred site, where Guillevic too had his own 'genesis'. Writing about the *Carnac* sequence, he remarks elsewhere: 'As a convinced materialist, I invoke the sacred. I dream of a society bathed in the sacred. For me, the poet must help others to live in the sacred in their daily lives.' A startlingly original, not to say unorthodox, vision of the final purposes of dialectical materialism! The menhirs, which recur frequently in the poem, are most obviously symbols of man's will to existence, uprightness, dignity, as well as enclosing a sacred site, where the elemental forces receive their due, and are appeased. They stand then, both in obeisance to, as well as in defiance against, the ocean, and as such reflect the poet's own divided allegiances. Whatever the truth, sea and menhirs are indissolubly connected for Guillevic. There is a violence at the heart of this liaison:

> De la mer aux menhirs,
> Des menhirs à la mer,
>
> La même route avec deux vents contraires
> Et celui de la mer
> Plein du meurtre de l'autre.
>
> From the sea to the menhirs,
> From the menhirs to the sea,
>
> The same road, two contrary winds
> With the one from the sea
> Full of the other's murder.

And a defiance:

> Il y a des milliers d'années
> Que les menhirs te tiennent tête
> Et à ce vent que tu leur jettes.
>
> For thousands of years
> The menhirs have faced you down
> And that wind you hurl at them.

But unlike the sea, the menhirs manifest a will to order, number, signification:

> Alignés, les menhirs,
> Comme si d'être en ligne
> Devait donner des droits.
>
> Aligned, the menhirs,
> As if being in line
> Should bestow rights.

And a quest for knowledge, an aspiration, a beseeching of something beyond them, alien to the sea:

> En imploration
> Comme les étoiles par tant de nuits
> Sont souvent les menhirs

Et la lune les fait
S'enquérir d'autres mondes,

Alors qu'au moins toi
On ne dirait pas.

Imploring,
Like the stars on so many nights
So often are the menhirs

And the moon makes them
Enquire about other worlds,

Whereas you at least
One wouldn't say.

Note in passing the laconic tone of that last remark addressed in almost throwaway style to the sea: it is a tone that recurs frequently in the poem, and by its lightness and discrete humour, saves the poem from a solemnity that might otherwise be crushing. (Towards the end of his life, Guillevic gave a series of interviews entitled *Humour-Terraqué*, with the express intention of emphasising the humour that is, indeed, central to his work, and in his opinion insufficiently noted by critics.)

Although they could fish, it was not from ploughing, sowing and reaping the sea that prehistoric man and his descendants could grow their crops – they turned and 'implored' the earth, instead. And yet, those who turned away, the poet acknowledges, cannot wholly exorcise the memory of the sea, finding resemblances and analogies in corn, grass and stone.

'La Fille' / 'The Girl'

There is, in Guillevic's work, an almost Beatrician presence, the *jeune fille*, whose name was Marie-Clotilde, and whom the poet loved between the ages of 13 and 17, when she died suddenly of meningitis. She is memorialised most explicitly in his 'Élégie', collected in *Sphère*, the book that followed *Carnac* in 1963. In *Vivre en poésie*, the poet talks about this early attachment as something so intense that he was dreaming about her half a century later. Marie-Clotilde represented, by her tenderness, if not the cure, then at least some compensation for the years of maternal neglect. In the same book, Guillevic speaks forthrightly, and magnificently of his love for women, which he does not hesitate to invest with a cosmic dimension that is almost Dantesque: 'If the woman you love is sacred, it's because you have, through her, a relationship with the cosmos. When she leaves you, the cosmos closes off.'

The figure of Marie-Clotilde, addressed simply as 'la fille', makes her appearance early on in *Carnac*, and she too represents a significant leitmotif, since it is with her, during her brief stay, that the poet is reconciled with the elemental forces around them (much as the virgin, and she alone, might tame the unicorn).

La fille qui viendrait	The girl who came
Serait la mer aussi,	Would also be the sea,
La mer parmi la terre.	The sea amidst the earth.

She can mediate between the poet's interior and the world 'out there'; she gathers, and distils aspects of the earth and the sea, just as, when she dies – as Guillevic movingly catalogues in 'Élégie' – those aspects will be scattered abroad once again, yet infused by her memory. As long as the girl is present, as mediatrix, the sea does not impinge oppressively, is in its place:

| Puisque le temps se tient | Since time limits itself |
| Aux dimensions de notre avoir. | To the dimensions of our possessions. |

Some features of the lost girl, her eyes that recalled the depths of the sea, or her 'smile of a seagull', that encircled him, are released at her death, to follow Guillevic's metaphoric process, back to the ocean. In the justly celebrated sections of *Carnac* where the poet casts earthly tributes upon the waters, when, in a remarkable inversion, he 'baptises' the sea with the various 'tastes' of the earth, or when he catalogues all the ingredients of the smell of Carnac earth, it is in part, I suspect, a further homage to Marie-Clotilde. It is at these moments that the poem breaks its strict, lapidary form and becomes almost a psalmodic, anaphoric incantation, a hymn to the material and multifariously incarnate world. It is likewise consistent with the memory of a beloved that in these sections the poet 'courts' the sea, much as a lover might, showering her with gifts, investing her with 'attributes'.

'Les Marais salants' / 'The Salt-pans'

The sea is also, of course, the poet's Muse. By turns flirtatious, capricious, tantrum-throwing, indifferent, like any muse. But there is a more strictly reflexive, metatextual, and even technical analogy that Guillevic draws early on in the poem, and it revolves around the salt-pans of his native Morbihan. Here the sea is channelled through a narrow conduit, known in French as an *étier*, into the marsh where it is reduced down to a sediment of salt. Guillevic develops the analogy in *Vivre en poésie* like this: 'And is the poet not the conduit which receives what it can of the world and preserves it in those little heaps of salt called poems?' Later on in his career, Guillevic entitled a collection *Étier* (1979), but it seems he first hit upon his analogy in *Carnac*. Apart from the sections devoted to Marie-Clotilde, the only moments in which he seems to have some mastery over the sea are in those describing the salt-pan:

> Là ça grouille dans toi,
> Mais au moins je le vois.

> There you are a-swarm
> But at least I can see.

But this apparent control leaves him uneasy and dissatisfied:

> Je t'ai prise à rebours
> Jusqu'aux marais salants

> Où je ne savais pas si je devais pleurer
> De n'avoir plus de toi que ces tas de sel blanc.

> I've tracked you backwards
> All the way to the salt marshes

> Where I don't know whether to cry,
> Possessing no more of you than these mounds of white salt.

It feels like a cheat or an illusion, and the poet seems to dismiss the possibility of "getting even" it offers, since it does not recur in the poem. There is, after all, no "getting even", and the sea, despite the passionate anthropomorphic pleadings delivered in the choicest language of the poet, remains at the end 'that trough / Definitive'. Many critics have noted a certain achieved serenity in *Carnac*, and it is true that the ubiquitous presence of fear, so palpable in *Terraqué*, is absent. But to what extent the alterity of the sea, the non-coincidence of subject and object remains an anguish, is finally a matter for each individual reader to decide.

STEPHEN ROMER
Nazelles, Val de Loire

Selected Bibliography

GUILLEVIC: **Poetry**

Terraqué (Paris: Gallimard, 1945).
Exécutoire (Paris: Gallimard, 1947).
Gagner (Paris: Gallimard, 1949).
Terre à bonheur (Paris: Seghers, 1952).
Trente-et-un sonnets (Paris: Gallimard, 1954).
Carnac (Paris: Gallimard, 1961).
Sphère (Paris: Gallimard, 1963).
Avec (Paris: Gallimard, 1966).
Euclidiennes (Paris: Gallimard, 1967).
Ville (Paris: Gallimard, 1969).
Paroi (Paris: Gallimard, 1970).
Encoches (Paris: Éditeurs français réunis, 1970).
Inclus (Paris: Gallimard, 1973).
Du domaine (Paris: Gallimard, 1977).
Étier (Paris: Gallimard, 1979).
Autres (Paris: Gallimard, 1980).
Trouées (Paris: Gallimard, 1981).
Requis (Paris: Gallimard, 1983).
Motifs (Paris: Gallimard, 1987).
Creusement (Paris: Gallimard, 1987).
Art poétique (Paris: Gallimard, 1989).
Le Chant (Paris: Gallimard, 1990).
Maintenant (Paris: Gallimard, 1993).
Possibles Futurs (Paris: Gallimard, 1996).

GUILLEVIC: **Prose (interviews)**

Vivre en poésie, with Lucie Albertini and Alain Vircondelet (Paris: Stock, 1980).
Choses Parlées, with Raymond Jean (Seysell: Champ Vallon, 1982).
Humour-Terraqué, with Jacques Lardoux (Paris: Presses Universitaires de Vincennes, 1997).

Selected further reading on Guillevic

Jean Tortel: *Guillevic*, in the series 'Poètes d'aujourd'hui' (Paris: Seghers, 1962).
Jean-Pierre Richard: 'Guillevic', in *Onze études sur la poésie moderne* (Paris: Seuil, 1964).

Philippe Jaccottet: *L'Entretien des Muses* (Paris: Gallimard, 1968).

Roger Munier: 'Face à face', on Guillevic, in *Critique*, 302 (Paris: Seuil, July 1972).

Jean Pierrot: *Guillevic ou la sérénité regagnée* (Seysell: Champ Vallon, 1984).

Guillevic: *Les chemins du poème*, special issue of the review *Sud* (Marseille: 1987).

Anne-Marie Mitchell: *Guillevic* (Paris: Le Temps parallèle, 1989).

Guillevic, special number of the review *Europe* (Paris: June-July, 1990).

Jean-Claude Pinson: *Habiter en poète* (Seysell: Champ Vallon, 1995).

Other References

Yves Bonnefoy: on 'Présence', see for example his *Entretiens sur la poésie* (Paris: Mercure de France, 1990); see also the introduction by Timothy Mathews to Bonnefoy's *On the Motion and Immobility of Douve* in the Bloodaxe Contemporary French Poets series (Newcastle upon Tyne: Bloodaxe Books, 1992).

Stéphane Mallarmé: *Pour un tombeau d'Anatole*, introduction by Jean-Pierre Richard (Paris: Seuil, 1961).

Michael Hamburger: *The Truth of Poetry* (Manchester: Carcanet, 1982; London: Anvil Press, reissue 1997).

Martin Heidegger: *Poetry, Language, Thought*, translated by Albert Hofstadter (New York: Harper Colophon, 1975).

A PERSONAL NOTE

If by chance you believe in the value of sounds
You should surely shiver
At the very name of sea.

My relationship with Eugène Guillevic began when we were Montparnasse neighbours. We shopped in the same market, Rue Daguerre; to see him press and smell a melon, or choose a pungent cheese, was a lesson in Gallic sensuousness. And he was so splendidly himself: smallish, thick-set, raucous-voiced, with the craggy dome of an intelligent simian, and a sudden smile which lit the beard and large glinting glasses. We liked each other instinctively, although for him English was the language of commerce, not romance. Like most modern French poets, he had contracted a mild form of Anglophobia, resenting the spread of English as a world language. (Deguy writes excitedly from China, declaring that at long last he has found a place where there is no trace of English, *les chiottes de la Cité Céleste!*)

I had translated one or two poems, as one does for a *confrère*, climbing *escalier C*, to the *douzième étage*, 11 rue Emile Dubois. I particularly liked 'Halts'.

During that halt which seemed to become eternal
Experience happened to us

And we always go out of these hidden cafés
Not quite the same as when we entered.

So far, so good, but I had not really come to grips with Guillevic's sparse, gnomic style, and thought he was well served anyway, by Denise Levertov's New Directions selection, and later by Teo Savory's Penguin edition.

Besides, my approach to even the translation of poetry is obsessive: I have to be fired. Or in this case, nearly drowned! Sailing home from Brittany, with my family, we found ourselves caught in a storm, Gale Force 9, with the wind rising. I have good sea legs, so it did not trouble me. Nor my little daughter, who scampered around happily as larger folk drooped. The dining-room and even the bar emptied, people turning green and hurrying out of sight. Soon I had the place to myself, except for my excited elfin companion, and the barman.

All I needed to keep going was a drink and a task. The task was simple: I had kept only one book from our luggage, a Gallimard paperback of Guillevic, including *Carnac*, which I now began to translate, using a French exercise book from Gibert. And as the great green waves heaved against the glass, I decided against either the black heaviness of Guinness, or the sting of spirits, opting instead for *pastis*. Soon the experience became hallucinatory, as the boat pitched, and the watered drink in my glass turned miraculously green.

> There you came vertical and green
> Rearing to touch our face.

I translated all of *Carnac* in those next days, without a dictionary, or anyone French near me. Becalmed in the Devil's Hole off Cornwall, I was joined in the bar by a scholar priest, bearing two books, his breviary, and a copy of the *Aeneid*. He smiled encouragingly as I chanted and pounded out rhythms to myself, under the doubled influence of Pernod and storm. The sea's rhythms pervaded night and day, and as a reward, in the same *cahier*, I recently found drafts of two of my own better poems, 'Crossing' and 'The Well Dreams'.

> The well dreams.
> Liquid bubbles.

Water, water everywhere, and quite a lot to drink! Clearly I was on a roll, in more ways than one, inspired by the hidden congruence between my own vision, and that of Guillevic, between somebody brought up beside the megaliths of Ireland, and another beside the stone alignments of Carnac. 'Sea, Stone, Woman, Land,' I wrote excitedly in my notebook, scrawling little drawings of the standing stones. It has taken me nearly 20 years to clean up the translation, but I hope this final version still echoes with some of that original excitement.

By the time I was finished I understood something of the mystic materialism which is at the heart of Guillevic's vision, the kind of Celtic communism you find also in the Shetland poems of Mac-Diarmid, like 'On a Raised Beach'. Guillevic's obsession with objects seems close to Ponge, but there is no hint of immanence, and he has compared the poet's craft to that of the carpenter. The precision of his procedures led him to write an extraordinary geometrical series a few years later, *Euclidiennes*. But that approach is already present in *Carnac*, for who else, regarding the ocean, would define it in terms of mathematics: 'A whole arithmetic / lies dead in your waves.'

JOHN MONTAGUE
Schull, Co. Cork

Carnac

Mer au bord du néant,
Qui se mêle au néant,

Pour mieux savoir le ciel,
Les plages, les rochers,

Pour mieux les recevoir.

*

Femme vêtue de peau
Qui façonnes nos mains,

Sans la mer dans tes yeux,
Sans ce goût de la mer que nous prenons en toi,

Tu n'excéderais pas
Le volume des chambres.

*

La mer comme un néant
Qui se voudrait la mer,

Qui voudrait se donner
Des attributs terrestres

Et la force qu'elle a
Par référence au vent.

*

Sea on the edge of nothingness,
Mingling with the nothingness,

Better to perceive the sky,
The beaches, the rocks,

Better to receive them.

*

Woman dressed in skin
You, who mould our hands

Without the sea in your eyes,
Without that sea-taste we seize in you,

You wouldn't overflow
The volume of rooms.

*

The sea, a nothingness
Which longs to be sea

Which longs to give itself
Terrestrial attributes

And the drive that it
Derives from the wind.

*

J'ai joué sur la pierre
De mes regards et de mes doigts

Et mêlées à la mer,
S'en allant sur la mer,
Revenant par la mer,

J'ai cru à des réponses de la pierre.

*

Ils ne sont pas tous dans la mer,
Au bord de la mer,
Les rochers.

Mais ceux qui sont au loin,
Égarés dans les terres,

Ont un ennui plus bas,
Presque au bord de l'aveu.

*

Ne te fie pas au goémon: la mer
Y a cherché refuge contre soi,
Consistance et figure.

Pourrait s'y dérouler
Ce qu'enroula la mer.

*

I played on the stone
With my stares, my fingers

And mingling with the sea,
Riding out on the sea,
Returning by sea,

I believed in answers from the stone.

                    *

They're not all in the sea,
On the shores of the sea,
Those rocks.

But those far off,
Straggling over the fields,

Have a deeper lassitude,
Near the brink of confession.

                    *

Don't trust the seaweed: the sea
Sought refuge there from itself,
Consistency and shape.

What the sea ravelled up
Might come unravelled there

                    *

Ne jouerons-nous jamais
Ne serait-ce qu'une heure,
Rien que quelques minutes,
Océan solennel,

Sans que tu aies cet air
De t'occuper ailleurs?

*

Je veux te préférer,
Incernable océan,

Les bassins que tu fais
Jusqu'aux marais salants.

Là je t'ai vu dormir
Avec d'autres remords.

*

D'abord presque pareille
À celle du grand large,

De bassin en bassin
Ton eau devient épaisse

Et finit par nourrir
Des espèces de vert

Comme font nos fontaines.

*

Will we never play,
If only for an hour,
A few fleeting minutes,
Solemn ocean,

Without you having that air
Of being busy elsewhere?

*

I want to prefer to you,
Unconfinable sea,

The pools you spread out
Into the salt marshes.

There I saw you asleep
Alongside other glooms.

*

Nearly the same at first
As the open sea.

From pool to pool
Your water thickens

And ends by nourishing
Forms of green

As our streams do.

*

Là ça grouille dans toi,
Mais au moins je le vois.

*

Depuis ton ouverture
Sur les rochers de Por en Dro
Vers le grand large et l'horizon,

Je t'ai prise à rebours
Jusqu'aux marais salants

Où je ne savais pas si je devais pleurer
De n'avoir plus de toi que ces tas de sel blanc.

*

Avant que tu sois là,
Collant à la saline,

Je t'ai vue bien souvent,
Cernée dans les bassins,

Rendre au soleil couchant
L'hommage des eaux calmes.

*

There you are a-swarm
But at least I can see.

*

From your cleft
In the rocks of Por en Dro
Out into the open sea, the horizon,

I've tracked you backwards
All the way to the salt marshes

Where I don't know whether to cry,
Possessing no more of you than these mounds of white salt.

*

Before you were there,
Clinging to the salt,

I saw you often
Confined to pools,

Return to the setting sun
The homage of calm waters.

*

Mais tu sais trop qu'on te préfère,
Que ceux qui t'ont quittée

Te trouvent dans les blés,
Te recherchent dans l'herbe,
T'écoutent dans la pierre,
Insaisissable.

*

Tu regardes la mer
Et lui cherches des yeux.

Tu regardes des yeux
Et tu y vois la mer.

*

À Carnac, derrière la mer,
La mort nous touche et se respire
Jusque dans les figuiers.

Ils sont dans l'air,
Les ossements.

Le cimetière et les dolmens
Sont apaisants.

*

But you know full well that we prefer you,
That those who've left you

Find you in the harvest,
Look for you in the grass,
Listen for you in the stone,
Unseizable.

*

You look at the sea
And search for its eyes

You look into eyes
And there see the sea.

*

At Carnac, behind the sea,
Death touches us, exhaling
As far as the fig trees.

They are in the air,
The bones of the dead.

The cemetery and the dolmens
Are soothing.

*

Mer sans vieillesse,
Sans plaie à refermer,
Sans ventre apparemment.

*

Église de Carnac
Qui est comme un rocher
Que l'on aurait creusé

Et meublé de façon
À n'y avoir plus peur.

*

Il y avait de pauvres maison
Et de pauvres gens.

Le temps
Pouvait n'être pas
Celui des vivants.

*

Ageless sea
With no wound to heal,
With no womb, apparently.

*

Church of Carnac
Like a rock
That has been hollowed

And furnished in a fashion
To banish fear.

*

There were poor houses
And poor people.

This couldn't be
A time
For the living.

*

Les gens y étaient comme des menhirs,
Ils étaient là depuis longtemps.

Ils n'allaient pas regarder la mer,
Ils écoutaient.

*

De la mer aux menhirs,
Des menhirs à la mer,

La même route avec deux vents contraires
Et celui de la mer
Plein du meurtre de l'autre.

*

Derrière les menhirs
Encore un autre vent
Sur des bois et des champs.

La terre et moins de sable,
C'est vert et c'est épais.

C'est de ce pays-là
Peut-être que la mer
Était un œil ouvert.

Ça se ressemble peu
Tout un corps et son œil.

*

The people dwelt there like menhirs,
They'd been there a long time.

They didn't go and stare at the sea,
They listened.

                    *

From the sea to the menhirs,
From the menhirs to the sea,

The same road, two contrary winds
With the one from the sea
Full of the other's murder.

                    *

Behind the menhirs
Yet another wind
On woods and fields.

The land, with less sand,
Is green, and lush.

It was from this land
Perhaps that the sea
Became an open eye.

It bears little resemblance
A whole body and its eye.

                    *

Tu es pour quelque chose
Dans la notion de Dieu,

Eau qui n'es plus de l'eau,
Puissance dépourvue de mains et d'instruments,

Pesanteur sans emploi
Pour qui le temps n'est pas.

*

Souvent pour t'occuper
Tu viens nous appeler
Vers la paix dans ton creux.

*

À ruminer tes fonds
Tu les surveilles mal,

Ou peut-être tu pousses
Ces monstres qui pénètrent
Dans le lieu de nos cauchemars.

*

You represent something
In the notion of God.

Water no longer water,
Power deprived of hands, instruments,

Weight without function
For which time doesn't exist.

*

Often to occupy yourself
You come calling us
Towards the peace in your hollow.

*

You so ponder your deeps
That you look after them poorly,

Or perhaps you encourage
Those monsters who penetrate
The place of our nightmares.

*

Soyons justes: sans toi
Que nous serait l'espace
Et que seraient les rocs?

*

Ta peur de n'être pas
Te fait copier les bêtes

Et ta peur de rater
Les mouvements des bêtes,
Leurs alarmes, leurs cris,
Te les fait agrandir.

Quelquefois tu mugis
Comme aucune d'entre elles.

*

Entre le bourg et la plage,
Il y avait sur la droite une fontaine

Qui n'en finissait pas
De remonter le temps.

*

Let's be fair: without you
What would space
And the rocks be for us?

*

Your fear of not being
Makes you imitate the beasts

And your fear of missing
The movement of beasts,
Their alarms, their cries,
Makes you magnify them.

Sometimes you roar
More than any of them.

*

On the right, between the town
And the beach, there was a stream

Perpetually
Rewinding time.

*

La fille qui viendrait
Serait la mer aussi,
La mer parmi la terre.

Le jour serait bonté,
L'espace et nous complices.

Nous apprendrions
À ne pas toujours partir.

*

Nous aurions la puissance
Et celle de n'en pas user.

Nous serions pleins
De notre avoir.

*

Présence alors jamais trop lourde
De vous autour de nous
À composer le monde,

Puisque le temps se tient
Aux dimensions de notre avoir.

*

48

The girl who came
Would also be the sea,
The sea amidst the earth.

The day would be bountiful,
Space and us accomplices.

We would learn
To not always part.

*

We would have power
And the power of not using it.

We would be full
Of what we possessed.

*

The presence then, never too heavy
Of you surrounding us
Composing our world,

Since time limits itself
To the dimensions of our possessions.

*

Elle avait un visage
Comme sont les visages
Ouverts et refermés
Sur le calme du monde.

Dans ses yeux j'assistais
Aux profondeurs de l'océan, à ses efforts
Vers la lumière supportable.

Elle avait un sourire égal au goéland.
Il m'englobait.

*

En elle s'affrontaient les rêves
Des pierres des murets,
Des herbes coléreuses,
Des reflets sur la mer,
Des troupeaux dans la lande.

Ils faisaient autour d'elle un tremblement
Comme le lichen
Sur les dolmens et les menhirs.

Elle vivait dessous,
M'appelait, s'appuyait
Sur ce que l'un à l'autre nous donnions.

Nos jours étaient fatals et gais.

*

She had a face
One of those faces
Open and closed on
The calm of the world.

In her eyes I shared
In the ocean depths, its struggle
Towards a tolerable light.

She had the smile of a seagull.
It encircled me.

*

In her clashed the dreams
Of low stone walls,
Potent herbs,
Sea shimmers,
Herds on the moors.

Around her a trembling
Like the lichen
On the dolmens and menhirs.

She lived underneath,
Called me, leaned on
What we gave to each other.

Our days were fatal and gay.

*

Ce qui fait que la morte est morte
Et moi vivant,

Ce qui fait que la morte
Se tient plus loin qu'auparavant,

Océan, tu te poses
Des questions de ce genre.

*

Quand je ne pensais pas à toi,
Quand je te regardais sans vouloir te chercher,

Quand j'étais sur tes bords
Ou quand j'étais dans toi,
Sans plus me souvenir de ta totalité,

J'étais bien,
Quelquefois.

*

And so the dead one is dead
And I go on living,

And so the dead one holds herself
Further off than before,

Ocean, you ask yourself
Such questions.

*

When I wasn't thinking about you,
When I watched you without seeking you,

When I was on your shores
Or when I was within you,
No longer remembering your entirety,

I felt fine,
Sometimes.

*

Bleu des jacinthes,
Bleu des profondeurs,

Il vient d'un feu faiseur de rouge
Qui tourne au violet puis au bleu.

Il est dans la terre.
Il nous cherche.

La mer
Peut l'ignorer.

*

Nous n'avons de rivage, en vérité,
Ni toi ni moi.

*

Écoute ce que fait
La poudre en explosant.

Écoute ce que fait
Le fragile violon.

*

Blue of hyacinths,
Blue of the deeps,

It comes from a light flaring red
Which turns to violet then to blue.

It is in the earth,
It seeks us.

The sea
Can ignore it.

*

We have no shore, really,
Neither you nor I.

*

Listen to what is done
By the powder exploding.

Listen to what is done
By the fragile violin.

*

Pas besoin de rire aussi fort,
De te moquer si fort
De moi contre le roc.

De toi je parle à peine,
Je parle autour de toi,

Pour t'épouser quand même
En traversant les mots.

*

Je sais qu'il y a d'autres mers,
Mer du pêcheur,
Mer des navigateurs,
Mer des marins de guerre,
Mer de ceux qui veulent y mourir.

Je ne suis pas un dictionnaire,
Je parle de nous deux

Et quand je dis la mer,
C'est toujours à Carnac.

*

No need to laugh so harshly,
To mock me so hard
Against the rock.

I hardly speak of you,
I speak around you,

To marry you all the same,
By wayfaring through words.

*

I know there are other seas,
Sea of the fisherman,
Sea of the navigators,
Sea of the men-o'-war,
Sea of those who wish to die therein.

I am not a dictionary,
I speak of us two

And when I say the sea,
It is always at Carnac.

*

Nulle part comme à Carnac,
Le ciel n'est à la terre,
Ne fait monde avec elle

Pour former comme un lieu
Plutôt lointain de tout
Qui s'avance au-dessous du temps.

*

Le vent vient de plus bas,
Des dessous du pays.

Le vent est la pensée
Du pays qui se pense
À longueur de sa verticale.

Il vient le vérifier, l'éprouver, l'exhorter,
À tenir comme il fait

Contre un néant diffus
Tapi dans l'océan
Qui demande à venir.

*

À Carnac d'autres vents
Font semblant d'apporter
Des souffles de vivants
Mais ne sont que passants.

*

Nowhere as at Carnac,
Does the sky touch the earth,
Make a world with it

To form a kind of place
Somehow far from everything
Which proceeds beneath time.

*

The wind comes from lower down,
From the nether land.

The wind is the thought
Of a country which defines itself
By its vertical length.

It comes to verify it, to test and exhort it,
To hold as it does

Against a diffuse nothingness
Lurking in the ocean
Which wants to come.

*

At Carnac other winds
Pretend to bear
Living breaths
But are only passers-by.

*

Les herbes de Carnac
Sur les bords du chemin
Sont herbes d'épopée
Que le repos ne réduit pas.

*

Du milieu des menhirs
Le monde a l'air

De partir de là,
D'y revenir.

La lumière y est bien,
Pardonne.

Le ciel
A trouvé sa place.

*

Fermes à l'écart, hameaux,
Dans vos pins,
Dans vos chemins,

Vous n'êtes pas tout à fait sûrs
De votre assise.

Le silence
Est obligatoire.

*

The grasses of Carnac
By the sides of the road
Are the growths of an epic
Which repose does not diminish.

*

From the middle of the menhirs
The world appears

To start from there,
And to return.

The light is fine there,
Forgives.

The sky
Has found its place.

*

Remote farms, hamlets,
Within your pines,
In your paths,

You are not fully sure
Of your situation.

Silence
Is obligatory.

*

61

Dans les terres,
Bien souvent,

La misère
Est au gris fixe.

*

Besoin d'un départ
Marquant les hameaux et les fermes

Vers la vie, davantage de vie,
Vers la mort.

Tremblement tous les jours
Entre les deux.

*

Sur la route de la plage, la fontaine
Était là comme venue d'ailleurs,
Mal habituée

– Ou c'était le reste.

*

In the fields,
Quite often,

The poverty
Is a constant grey.

*

A need for departure
Marking the hamlets and farms

Towards life, further life,
Towards death.

A trembling every day
Between the two.

*

On the road to the beach, the stream was there
As though come from elsewhere,
Ill at ease

– Or everything else was.

*

Parfois il y avait au large
Des lézards gris dormant
Sous une longue fumée.

La vue de l'escadre
Faisait du pays de Carnac
Un verre de lampe qui peut être cogné.

*

Avoue, soleil:
C'est toi l'étendue.

Avec de la mer,
Ça te réussit.

Tu sais comme on peut
Apporter du vague
Au milieu du net
Et la mer s'y prête.

*

Sometimes off the coast there were
Sleeping grey lizards
Under a long haze.

The view from the prow
Made the land of Carnac
A lamp globe which could be struck.

*

Admit, sun:
You are the sprawler.

Along with the sea,
It works for you.

You know how one can
Bring the vague
Into the midst of the definite
And the sea goes along with it.

*

Sans toi d'ailleurs, soleil,
La mer serait encore
Cognant à l'infini,
Mais alors dans ce noir

Qu'on suspecte la mer
De vouloir devenir

Quand tu es là,
Soleil.

*

Amis, ennemis,
Le soleil, la mer,

Fatigués l'un de l'autre, habitués,
Mais décidés soudain

À dépasser enfin l'extrême du désir
Qu'ils savent, chacun d'eux,
Pouvoir atteindre sans se perdre au sein de l'autre.

Décidés à savoir
Ce qu'ils seront alors

Si la chose arrive
Que l'autre les prenne.

*

Without you, indeed, sun,
The sea would still be
Striking at the infinite,
But in the dark

One suspects the sea
Of wishing to become

When you are there,
Sun.

*

Friends, enemies,
The sun, the sea,

Fatigued with each other, regulars,
But suddenly decided

To push finally beyond the extremity of desire
Which they know, each of them,
How to attain without drowning themselves in the other's embrace.

Determined to learn
What they will then be

If it happens
That the other seizes them.

*

Soleil sur la mer,
Silence, un point fixe

Auquel vous tendez
Le soleil, la mer –

Et l'air qui se perd
À vous distinguer!

*

Le soleil, la mer,
Lequel de vous deux
Prétend calmer l'autre,

Au moyen de quoi?

*

Vous voulez vous battre
Et vous n'arrivez à vous rencontrer
Que pour vous frôler.

*

Sun on the sea,
Silence, a fixed point

Towards which you tend
The sun, the sea –

And the air which vanishes
In making you out!

*

The sun, the sea,
Which of you two
Claims to calm the other,

By what means?

*

You want to fight each other
And you only manage to meet
To chafe each other.

*

Au moins tu sais, toi, océan,
Qu'il est inutile
De rêver ta fin.

       *

Oui, je t'ai vue sauvage, hors de ta possession,
Devant endosser les assauts du vent.

Je t'ai vue bafouée, recherchant ta vengeance
Et la faisant porter sur d'autres que le vent.

Mais je parle de toi quand tu n'es que toi-même,
Sans pouvoir que d'absorber.

       *

« Désossée », « dégraissée »,
Ce sont des voix.

« Décolorée »,
« Grise, grise, grise »,
C'est une autre voix.

Elles t'en veulent, ces voix,
Elles sont dans le vent, dans le soleil,
Dans ta couleur, dans ta masse.

       *

At least you, ocean, you know
That it is futile
To dream your ending.

*

Yes, I have seen you, wild, out of control,
Before shouldering the assaults of the wind.

I have seen you flouted, seeking your revenge
And wreaking it on others than the wind.

But I speak of you when you are only yourself,
Without power except to absorb.

*

'Filleted', 'fatless',
Say some voices.

'Bleached out',
'Grey, grey, grey',
That's another voice.

They have it in for you, those voices,
They are in the wind, in the sun,
In your colour, in your mass.

*

C'est bon, n'est-ce pas?
De lécher le pied des rochers,
Ça te change de toi.

*

Sur la plage et les terres
Le soleil se rattrape.

Là il est maître et là
Ce n'est pas lui qu'il voit
Autant que dans la mer.

Là, il se voit le père.

*

À Carnac, le linge qui sèche
Sur les ajoncs et sur les cordes

Retient le plus joyeux
Du soleil et du vent.

Appel peut-être
À la musique.

*

It's good, isn't it?
To lick the foot of rocks,
That's a change for you.

*

On the beach and the land
The sun recovers himself

There he is master and there
It is not himself he sees
As much as in the sea.

There, he sees himself as the father.

*

At Carnac, the linen which dries
On the gorse and on the lines

Retains the greatest joy
Of the sun and the wind.

A summons perhaps
To music.

*

Il y a dans les cours de fermes
Du purin qui ne s'en va pas

Et c'est pour leur donner
De l'épaisseur terrestre.

*

Que dis-tu de ce bleu
Que tu deviens sur les atlas?

As-tu parfois rêvé
De ressembler à ça?

*

On ne peut pas te boire,
Tu refuses nos corps.

Mais on te touche
Un peu.

On a ton goût surtout
Et ton odeur qui fait
S'agrandir la distance

Et parfois s'engouffrer
Dans le temps de tes origines.

*

In the courtyards of farms there is
A slurry that doesn't go away

And it is to give them
The density of earth.

*

What do you say of this blue
You become on the atlas?

Have you sometimes dreamt
Of looking like that?

*

One cannot drink you,
You refuse our bodies.

But one can touch you
A little.

We have your taste above all
And your odour which makes
The distance unfurl

And sometimes plunge back
Into the time of your origins.

*

Tu peux être fraîche
Et douce à la peau
Dans les jours d'été,

Mais tu ne parles pas
Des souvenirs communs d'il y a quelque temps,
Comme fait la source.

*

On peut plonger en toi.

Tu l'acceptes très bien,
Même tu le demandes.

Mais ce n'est que toucher
Un passé légendaire
Qui s'oublie dans ta masse

Dont tu parais absente.

*

Cet homme que tu prends,
Tu en as bientôt fait,
Au bout de quelques mètres,
Un objet simple et blanc

Qui n'a pour avenir
Que d'être plus défait

Au rythme régulier
De la tranquille exécution de tes sentences.

*

You can be fresh
And soft to the skin
In the days of summer,

But you don't speak
Of shared memories of a while ago,
As the wellspring does.

*

One can plunge into you.

You accept it very well,
You even ask for it.

But it is only to touch
A legendary past
Which loses itself in your mass

From which you seem absent.

*

That man you take,
You have soon made of him,
After a few metres,
An object simple and white

Which has no future
But to be further undone

To the regular rhythm
Of your sentences' tranquil execution.

*

Prise entre des rochers
Au cours de la marée,
Tu t'y plais, on dirait.

Douce, douce, caressante –
Et c'est peut-être vrai.

*

Ils n'ont pas l'air de te comprendre,
Ceux qui vivent dans toi,
Ceux qui sont faits de toi,
Ces poissons, ces crevettes.

*

Il me semble pourtant
Qu'à bien les regarder,
Les toucher, les manger.

Ils nous disent de toi
Ce qu'on ne saurait pas,

Qu'ils nous disent surtout
Ce que tu sens de toi.

*

Caught between the rocks
In the course of the tide,
You are happy, one might say.

Soft, soft, caressing –
And it is, perhaps, true.

*

They don't seem to understand you,
Those who live in you,
Those who are made from you,
Those fish, those shrimp.

*

It seems to me though
That looking at them well,
Touching them, eating them,

They tell us about you
What we didn't know,

What they tell us above all
Is how you feel about yourself.

*

Tu n'as pour te couvrir
Que le ciel évasé,

Les nuages sans poids
Que du vent fait changer.

Tu rêvais de bien plus,
Tu rêvais plus précis.

*

Toujours les mêmes terres
À caresser toujours.

Jamais un corps nouveau
Pour t'essayer à lui.

*

L'insidieux est notre passé,
Chargé sur nous de représailles.

Pourquoi faut-il que l'on t'y trouve,
Océan, accumulation?

*

You have nothing to cover yourself with
But the flaring sky,

The weightless clouds
Which the wind changes.

You dreamt of much more,
You dreamt more strictly.

*

Always the same lands
To caress always.

Never a new body
To have a go at him.

*

The insidious is our past,
Heavy on us with reprisals.

Why does one have to find in you,
Ocean, accumulation?

*

Quand tu reçois la pluie
Reconnais-tu ta fille?

Exilée, revenue,
Ignorant son histoire,

Qui croit qu'elle te frappe
Ou peut-être t'apaise.

*

Contre le soleil
Tu as voulu t'unir,

Mais avec quoi,
Sauf avec lui?

*

Si l'espace une fois
Brûlait en rouge et bleu
Mais plus loin, sur la terre,

Ce serait ta fête.

Tu pourrais être douce, après.

*

When you receive the rain
Do you recognise your daughter?

Exiled, back again,
Oblivious of her history,

Believing that she strikes you
Or perhaps soothes you.

*

Against the sun
You have wished to unite,

But with what,
If not the sun?

*

If space once
Burned in red and blue
But farther, on the land,

You would celebrate.

You could be gentle, after.

*

Tu ne changeras pas au cours des ans,
Même si tu en rêves à coups de vagues.

Mais pour moi d'autres jours
Pourraient venir de mon vivant.

Ce sera comme un cercle
Qui se réveille droite,

Une équation montée
Dans l'ordre des degrés,

D'autres géométries
Pour vivre la lumière.

Alors, que seras-tu pour moi?
Que dirons-nous?

*

Alors, j'irai
Vers le total moi-même.

Ma paix sera plus grande
Et voudra te gagner.

*

Les profondeurs, nous les cherchons,
Est-ce les tiennes?

Les nôtres ont pouvoir de flamme.

*

You will not change in the course of the years,
Even if you dream of it to the beat of waves.

But for me other days
Could come in my lifetime.

It would be like a circle
Which wakens up straight,

An equation mounting
In a series of degrees,

Of other geometries
To quicken the light.

Then, what will you be for me?
What shall we say?

*

So, I will go
Towards my total self.

My peace will be greater
And will seek to win you.

*

The depths, we search for them,
Are they yours?

Ours have flame's power.

*

Même assis sur la terre
Et regardant la terre,

Il n'est pas si facile
De garder sa raison
Des assauts de la mer.

*

En somme, avec toi,
Qu'on soit sur tes bords,
Qu'on te voie de loin

Ou qu'on soit entré
Te faire une cour
Que la courbe impose
Où sont le soleil, le ciel et le sol,

N'importe où qu'on soit,
On est à la porte.

*

On est à la porte,
On a l'habitude,
On ne s'y fait pas.

*

Even sitting on the ground
And looking at the ground,

It is not so easy
To protect one's reason
From the assaults of the sea.

*

To sum up, with you,
Whether one is on your shores,
Or whether one sees you from afar

Or whether one has entered
To pay court to you
As by the curve demanded
Where are the sun, the sky and the soil,

No matter where one is,
One is at the doorway.

*

We are at the door,
We are used to it,
We cannot get used to it.

*

À la porte de l'océan
Et parlant, parlant.

Le difficile,
C'est d'être lui

Et si tu l'étais
C'est de rester toi,

Assez pour savoir
Que tu es les deux

Et pour en crier.

*

Cogne, cogne, cogne,
Puisque ça t'occupe

Et puisque pour nous
Le spectacle est grand.

*

On comprend bien
Que ça t'obsède

D'être un jour dressée
À la verticale
Au-dessus des terres.

On comprend bien.

*

At the ocean's door
And speaking, speaking.

The difficult thing
Is to be the ocean

And if you were
To remain yourself,

Enough to know
That you are both

And to shout it out.

*

Pound, pound, pound,
Since that keeps you busy

And since for us
The spectacle is grand.

*

One understands well
That you are obsessed

With standing, one day,
Upright, vertical
Over the earth.

One understands well?

*

Tu rêves des rochers
Pour t'en faire un squelette.

Continue, continue,
Flatte-les de tes vagues

Et reste invertébrée.

*

Beaucoup d'hommes sont venus,
Sont restés. Terre d'ossements,
Poussière d'ossements.

Il y avait donc
L'appel de Carnac.

Comment chantaient-ils,
Ceux des menhirs?

Peut-être est-ce là
Qu'ils avaient moins peur.

Centre du ciel et de la mer,
De la terre aussi,
La lumière le dit.

Chantant, eux,
Pas loin de la mer,
Pour être admis par la lumière.

Regardant la mer,
Lui tournant le dos,
Implorant la terre.

*

You dream of rocks
To fashion yourself a skeleton.

Go on, go on,
Caress them with your waves

And remain invertebrate.

*

Many men have come,
Have stayed. Land of bones,
Powdered bones.

Thus there was
The call of Carnac.

How did they sing
The menhir-people?

Perhaps it was there
They knew less fear.

Centre of the sky and of the sea,
Of the land as well,
The light says it.

Singing, they were,
Not far from the sea,
To be let in by the light.

Beholding the sea,
Turning their back on it,
Imploring the land.

*

Il arrive qu'un pin
Du haut de la falaise
Te regarde et frissonne
Tant que dure le jour.

*

Il y a des moments
Où l'on peut s'endormir
Même tout près de toi
Sans te manquer d'égard.

Ce sont peut-être ceux
Qu'un grand calme t'inflige,

Quand tu as fait tes comptes
Et les as trouvés bons.

Il arrive à chacun,
Même à toi, forcenée,
D'être content de soi.

*

Calme, calme et contente
D'avoir fait ton bilan.

Horizontale et l'acceptant,
Le temps que tu savoures
Les postes de l'actif.

*

It happens that a pine
From the top of the cliff
Looks at you and quivers
All day long.

*

There are the moments
When one could drowse off
Even right beside you
Without lack of respect.

Those are the moments, perhaps,
A great calm inflicts on you,

When you have settled your accounts
And found them good.

Everyone sometimes,
Even you, with your frenzy,
Can be pleased with themselves.

*

Calm, calm and content
That you have taken stock.

Horizontal and accepting it,
The season when you savour
Action's station.

*

Le désert et toi –
C'est le sable.

La montagne et toi, la haute montagne,
C'est le vent.

Mais dans le désert,
Dans le vent sur la montagne,

Elle n'y est pas,
Ta volonté.

*

Ruminant, toi,
Rabâchant, rabâchant,

Quand les coquelicots
Ne parlaient que de vivre.

*

Pas délicate,
Pas difficile,
Pas assez femme.

Tu prends tout,
Parfois tu rejettes.

*

The desert and you –
The domain of sand.

The mountain and you, the high mountain,
The domain of wind.

But in the desert,
In the mountain wind,

It doesn't exist –
Your will.

*

Ruminating, you,
Chewing, chewing the cud,

When the poppies
Spoke only of living.

*

Not delicate,
Not difficult,
Not woman enough.

You take everything,
Sometimes you throw it back.

*

Sans corps,
Mais épaisse.

Sans ventre,
Mais molle.

Sans oreilles,
Mais parlant fort.

Sans peau,
Mais tremblante.

*

Pour garder tes nuits,
As-tu supplié
Parfois les rochers?

*

Si vaste, si lourde
Et si limitée.

Un peu de sable
Que tu remues.

Il te faut longtemps
Pour bien peu de chose.

*

Without body,
But bulky.

Without belly,
But soft.

Without ears,
But loud-speaking.

Without skin,
But a-tremble.

*

Have you implored
The rocks sometimes
To guard your nights?

*

So vast, so heavy
And so limited.

A little sand
Which you shift.

You need so long
To do so very little.

*

On dirait que ça te répugne
De mouiller ce que tu touches.

Comme si c'était
Te donner trop.

*

Allez donc! Allez!
Trêve de nos pointes.

Paix sur toi, la grande,
Et paix sur nous.

On ne se dit rien,
On s'ignore, on va
Chacun dans sa loi.

Tu veux qu'on essaye
En feignant de croire
Que ce soit possible?

*

Trop large
Pour être chevauchée.

Trop large
Pour être étreinte.

Et flasque.

*

One would think it disgusts you
To moisten what you touch.

As if it were
To give of yourself too much.

*

Go on then! Go!
A truce on our headlands.

Peace to you, great one,
And peace to us.

We don't speak to each other,
We ignore each other, we go
Each one his own way.

Would you like us to try
Feigning to believe
That it is possible?

*

Too vast
To be straddled.

Too vast
To be hugged.

And flaccid.

*

Je te baptise
Du goût de la pierre de Carnac,
Du goût de la bruyère et de la coquille d'escargot,
Du goût de l'humus un peu mouillé.

Je te baptise
Du goût de la bougie qui brûle,
Du goût du lait cru,
Du goût différent de plusieurs jeunes filles,
Du goût de la pomme verte et de la pomme très mûre.

Je te baptise
Du goût du fer qui commence à rouiller,
Du goût d'une bouche et d'une langue avides,
Du goût de la peau que tu n'as pas salée,
Du goût des bourgeons, des jeunes girolles.

– C'est sans effet sur toi, oui.
C'était pour moi.

*

Balayure de roses,
Corne de chèvrefeuille,
Galet d'églantine,
Pépin de joue pâle,
Rayons de vin,
Sourires de viscère,
Éperons d'étoupe,
Éclairs de marbre,

Ça ne te dit rien, n'est-ce pas?
Ça n'a pas de rapports avec toi?

I baptise you
With the taste of stone at Carnac,
With the taste of heather and the snail's shell,
With the taste of moist loam.

I baptise you
With the taste of the candle that burns,
With the taste of new milk,
With the differing taste of several young girls,
With the taste of the green apple and the overripe.

I baptise you
With the taste of iron beginning to rust,
With the taste of an avid mouth and tongue,
With the taste of the skin you have not salted,
With the taste of buds, of young wild mushrooms.

– It has no effect on you, of course.
This was for me.

*

Seawrack of roses,
Horn of honeysuckle,
Shingle of dog rose,
Pip of pallid cheek,
Arrays of wine,
Smiles of innards,
Spurs of oakum,
Glimmers of marble,

That means nothing to you, does it?
That has nothing to do with you?

Pas moins d'ailleurs
Que les autres choses
Que je dis de toi?

Je crois que si.

*

Ne t'énerve pas, ne te laisse pas
Noyauter, vider,
Seconde après seconde.

Prends ces moments
L'un après l'autre. Épuise-les.
Fais-toi. Fais
Ton contentement.

Ou crie et souffre, crie,
Mais pas ce creux
Qui prend du volume.

Comprends que je sais.

*

Pas plus seul qu'un autre
Au sein de ta masse,
Devant ta masse,
Pas plus veuf qu'un autre,

Mais sans programme,
Sans ouvrage.

*

Not less anyhow
Than the other things
I say about you?

I think it does.

*

Don't get irritated, don't let yourself
Get pipped, drained,
Second by second.

Take these moments
One after another. Exhaust them.
Be yourself. Make
Your peace.

Or cry and suffer, cry
But not this hollow
That gathers volume.

Understand that I know.

*

No more alone than another
In the bosom of your mass,
Before your bulk,
No more forlorn than another,

But without a plan,
Without a task.

*

Pas absente du vent
Quand le vent se dépasse

Et fait autour de nous
Un creux pareil au tien.

Pas absente du vent –
Ou c'est ton souvenir.

*

Infatigable, fatiguée –

Mais quelle est l'epithète
Qui ne te conviendrait?

*

Ton père:
Le silence.

Ton devoir:
Le mouvement.

Ton refus:
La brume.

Tes rêves.

*

Not away from the wind
When the wind whips up

And makes around us
A hollow like yours.

Not away from the wind –
Or it is a memory of you.

*

Indefatigable, fatigued –

But what adjective
Does not suit you?

*

Your father:
Silence.

Your duty:
Movement.

Your disavowal:
Mist.

Your dreams.

*

Toi, sans abri
Contre le vent, bien sûr,
Et contre le soleil
Qui affûte les heures,

Sans rien pour le voiler
La procession des astres
Et leurs cérémonies
De longue adoration.

*

Sous nos pieds la terre,
Comme si de rien n'était.

Toi, l'indifférence
Ne t'est pas donnée.

*

Je suis des tiens, va!

Tout bien pesé,
Tout bien aimé,
Tout bien maudit,

Je suis des tiens.

*

You, without shelter
Against the wind, of course,
And against the sun
Which whets the hours,

With nothing to veil from you
The procession of stars
And their ceremonies
Of long adoration.

*

The earth under our feet,
As if 'twere nothing.

To you, indifference
Is not given.

*

I am one of yours, you know!

All well weighed,
All well loved,
All well cursed,

I am one of yours.

*

Il s'est passé quelque chose à Carnac,
Il y a longtemps.

Quelque chose qui compte
Et tu dis, lumière,

Qu'il y a lieu
D'en être fier.

*

Maisons blanches, vous de Carnac,
À tendre votre chaux contre qui veut dormir,

Vous la fin de la terre
Et la fin de la mer,

Où le soleil enfin
Ne peut plus s'étaler,

Mais cogne, mer,
Comme tu fais.

*

Autant que les maisons,
Les gens s'abandonnaient.

Il y avait parfois tant de vent
Que le temps n'était pas pesant.

Mais le vent
Camouflait le temps.

*

Something happened at Carnac
A long time ago.

Something which matters
And you say, light,

There is reason
To be proud of it.

*

White houses of Carnac,
Your whitewash outspread against those who would sleep,

You land's end
And the end of the sea,

Where the sun at last
Can no longer flaunt itself,

But pound, sea,
As is your wont.

*

As well as the houses,
The people gave in.

Sometimes there was so much wind
That the weather did not oppress.

But the wind
Disguised the weather.

*

Si par hasard tu crois à la valeur des sons
Tu dois bien frissonner
À ce seul nom de mer.

*

Puissante par moments
De force ramassée
Comme pour un travail,

Claquant contre le roc
Et tombant lourdement,

Quelquefois projetée
Comme un vomissement.

*

Pardonne-moi si le caillou
Ramassé dans un coin de terre,

Même sur un sentier
Piétiné, harassé,

Me parle plus
Que tes galets, parfois.

*

If by chance you believe in the value of sounds
You should surely shiver
At the very name of sea.

*

Powerful at moments
Of mustered force
As for a task

Crashing against the rocks
And falling heavily,

Sometimes spewed
Like a vomit.

*

Pardon me if a pebble
Gathered in an earthy corner

Even on a path
Trampled, trodden

Speaks to me more
Than your shingle, sometimes.

*

Crois-tu qu'il t'aime, le sable,
Qui sans toi serait debout
Dans le roc qui te domine,

Alors qu'il te sert de lieu
Où tu viens te promener?

*

Entre la mer et la terre
Cultivée, arrangée,

La lande fait la transition
Et plaide pour ne pas choisir.

*

Tu devrais être la première
À comprendre et savoir
Que l'on aime la terre,

Que l'on peut préférer
Y vivre loin de toi.

*

Le vent, le sable et toi
Aviez des rendez-vous

Dont vous faisiez semblant
De parler en passant.

*

Do you believe he loves you, the sand,
Who, without you, would be up there
On the rock looming over you,

While he serves as a place
Where you come for a stroll?

*

Between the sea and the land
Tilled, tidied,

The moors make the transition
And plead for not choosing.

*

You should be the first
To understand and know
That one loves the land,

That one can prefer
To live far from you.

*

The wind, the sand and you
Had rendezvous

Of which you pretended
To speak in passing.

*

Il y a des milliers d'années
Que les menhirs te tiennent tête
Et à ce vent que tu leur jettes.

*

Remue, dors ou remue
L'horloge va sa loi,

Plus parente de toi
Que l'horloge ne croit.

*

Vraisemblablement,
Sans toi, l'océan,

Ils n'auraient rien fait à Carnac,
Ceux des menhirs.

*

Je me suis souvent demandé
Ce que tu pensais des couleurs.

Je sens que la question te gêne,
Mais remarque:

Jamais l'idée ne m'est venue
De la poser à l'hortensia

*

For thousands of years
The menhirs have faced you down
And that wind you hurl at them.

*

Stir, sleep and stir
The clock follows its law

Being more your kin
Than the clock lets on.

*

Probably
Without you, ocean,

They would have done nothing at Carnac,
The men of the menhirs.

*

I have often wondered
What you thought of colours.

I sense the question bothers you,
But mark:

I never ever thought
Of putting it to the hortensia.

*

Si tu pouvais nous dire
Au moins sur le passage
Du gris glauque au bleu vert.

C'est qu'on n'y comprend guère
À seulement te regarder.

Il faudrait être ton amant.

*

Il y a des hommes
Qui ne voient en toi que la nourricière.

Je les envie peut-être,
Car j'aime aussi
Prendre un crabe qui court
Ou sortir des poissons,

Mais j'ai bien un peu peur
Que ce que j'aime alors
Soit de l'ordre de la revanche.

*

Quand tu parais dormir,
Vaincue par le soleil,
Ta fatigue ou les songes,

Alors le goéland
Crie durement pour toi.

*

If you could tell us
At least about the passage
From glaucous grey to blue-green.

You see, we can't really understand
From only looking at you.

One would have to be your lover.

*

There are men
Who see in you only the fish harvest.

I envy them perhaps,
For I too love
To grasp a crawly crab
Or lift out fish,

But I am a little afraid
That what I love then
Might be bound up with revenge.

*

When you seem to sleep,
Stupefied by the sun,
Your weariness or reveries,

Then the seagull
Cries harshly for you.

*

Ne va pas croire
Que le spectacle que tu donnes
Soit toujours suffisant.

On peut être assis sur tes bords,
Vivre tes vagues, la marée,

Regarder le complot
Que vous mettez au point,
Toi, l'air et l'horizon,

Déplorer que jamais
Tu ne sois là t'ouvrant,
Montrant tes profondeurs,

Et ne pas toujours
Être intéressé.

*

Je te parle et je suis
Obligé de le faire.

Je te parle et je fais
Comme si quelquefois
Tu m'entendais parler.

Je te parle et dis-moi
Si tu comprends pourquoi.

*

Now, do not think
That the show you put on
Is always enough.

One can sit on your shores
Absorb your waves, the tide,

Watch the plot
That you weave,
You, the air and the horizon,

Deplore that you never
Are there, revealing yourself,
Showing your depths,

And not always
Be interested.

*

I speak to you and
Am obliged to do so.

I speak to you and make
Believe that sometimes
You hear me speak.

I speak to you and tell me
If you understand why.

*

Alignés, les menhirs,
Comme si d'être en ligne
Devait donner des droits.

*

En imploration
Comme les étoiles par tant de nuits
Sont souvent les menhirs

Et la lune les fait
S'enquérir d'autres mondes,

Alors qu'au moins toi
On ne dirait pas.

*

Sois ici remerciée
De n'être pas pareille à nous

Dont le rêve est toujours
D'être réconciliés

Quand pourtant
Ce n'est pas possible.

*

Aligned, the menhirs,
As if being in line
Should bestow rights.

*

Imploring,
Like the stars on so many nights
So often are the menhirs

And the moon makes them
Enquire about other worlds,

Whereas you at least
One wouldn't say.

*

Be thanked here
For not being like us

Whose dream is always
To be reconciled

When surely
It is not possible.

*

J'écris de toi dans un pays
Où le végétal
Ne cesse d'attaquer
Comme si c'était toi
Qui grondais jusqu'ici.

*

Les menhirs sont en rang
Vers quelque chose
Qui doit avoir eu lieu.

*

À Carnac, l'odeur de la terre
A quelque chose de pas reconnaissable.

C'est une odeur de terre
Peut-être, mais passée
À l'échelon de la géométrie

Où le vent, le soleil, le sel,
L'iode, les ossements, l'eau douce des fontaines,
Les coquillages morts, les herbes, le purin,
La saxifrage, la pierre chauffée, les détritus,
Le linge encore mouillé, le goudron des barques,
Les étables, la chaux des murs, les figuiers,
Les vieux vêtements des gens, leurs paroles,
Et toujours le vent, le soleil, le sel,
L'humus un peu honteux, le goémon séché,

I write about you in a country
Where the plant life
Ceaselessly attacks
As if it were you
Grumbling this far.

*

The menhirs are ranked
Towards something
Which must have happened.

*

At Carnac, the smell of the earth
Has something not recognisable.

It is an odour of earth
Perhaps, but transferred
To the level of geometry.

Where the wind, the sun, the salt
The iodine, the bones, the sweet water of streams,
The dead seashells, the grasses, the slurry,
The saxifrage, the warmed stone, the bilge,
The still-wet linen, the tar of boats,
The byres, the whitewashed walls, the fig trees,
The old clothes of the people, their speech,
And always the wind, the sun, the salt,
The slightly disgusting loam, the dried seaweed,

Tous ensemble et séparément luttent
Avec l'époque des menhirs

Pour être dimension.

*

Femme, femme, au secours
Contre le souvenir
Enrôleur de la mer.

Mets près de moi
Ton corps qui donne.

*

Toujours nouvelle – et pas
Parce que tu changes.

Toujours nouvelle
Puisque je t'apprends
Et jamais ne sais ce que tu seras.

Donc tu donnes, quand même,
Tu ouvres.

*

All together and separately struggle
With the epoch of the menhirs

To measure up.

*

Woman, woman, to the rescue
Against the remembered
Blandishments of the sea.

Press close to me
Your giving body.

*

Always new – and not
Because you change.

Always new
For I study you
And never know what you will be.

So you give, nonetheless,
You open up.

*

Donne au moins ce qu'en toi
Nous avons investi.

Pour remplacer ce Dieu
Où nous t'avons jetée,

Nous avons besoin
De trouver la fête.

– Il ne semble pas
Que tu aies la tienne.

*

Pour se faufiler
Dans l'étroit canal
Qui menait au port avant les bassins,

Elles se pressaient, tes vagues,
Lors de la marée,
Elles se bousculaient.

Elles avaient besoin
Que l'interminable
Soit fini pour elles.

*

Give at least what we
Have invested in you.

To replace that God
Where we have thrown you,

We have need
To find a feast day.

– You would not seem
To have your own.

*

To sneak into
The narrow canal
Leading to the port before the docks,

They hurried, your waves,
At the time of the tide,
They bustled along.

They needed
That the endless
Be ended for them.

*

Je parle mal de toi.

Il me faudrait parler
Aussi vague et confus
Que rabâchent tes eaux.

Et des éclats
Pour ta colère,

Tes idées fixes
Sous le soleil.

*

Je n'ai jamais compris
Pourquoi, où qu'ils soient,
Toujours les gens causaient

Et rarement
j'ai su de quoi.

Tu fais comme eux,
Tu veux causer,
Tu te racontes.

*

I speak badly of you.

I should speak
As vague and confusedly
As your monotonous waters.

And in bursts
For your anger,

Your fixed ideas
Under the sun.

*

I have never understood
Why, wherever they are,
People always chatter

And I have rarely
Known what about.

You do as they do,
You want to chat,
You tell your tale.

*

Ce qu'aussi tu veux
C'est t'allonger jusque dans les terres,
C'est les pénétrer, c'est être avec l'herbe.

Tu fais des rivières,
De vieux marais.

Mais là tu te perds
En perdant ta masse

Et ce néant
Qui te traverse.

*

Toute une arithmétique
Est morte dans tes vagues.

*

Il y a des moments
Où l'on te trouve entière,
Brutale d'être toi.

Là tu viens verticale et verte te dresser
À toucher notre face.

Là tu nais en toi-même
À chaque instant que nous faisons.

*

Something else you want
Is to unfurl yourself as far as the fields,
To enter them, to be with the grass.

You make rivers,
Ancient marshes

But there you lose yourself,
Losing your mass

And that nothingness
Which courses through you.

*

A whole arithmetic
Lies dead in your waves.

*

There are moments
When one finds you whole,
Brutally yourself.

There you come vertical and green
Rearing to touch our face.

There you renew yourself
Every instant that we exist.

*

Parfois tu étais
Un moment de moi.

Je nous exposais
Au risque d'aller,

Car plus tard
Est toujours présent.

*

Quand je te regardais jusqu'au plus loin possible,
C'est vers le midi
Que je me tournais.

Je l'ai su depuis,
Lumière extasiée,
Horizon vaincu.

*

Il me semble parfois
Qu'entre nous il y a
Le souvenir confus
De crimes en commun.

Nous voici projetés face à face
Pour comprendre.

*

Sometimes you were
A moment of me.

I exposed us
To the risk of succeeding,

For later
Is always present.

*

When I watched you as far away as possible,
It was towards noon
That I turned.

I have known it since,
Rapturous light,
The horizon overcome.

*

Sometimes it seems to me
That between us there is
The confused memory
Of crimes in common.

See us now, thrown face to face
So as to comprehend.

*

Avant nous
Tu étais là,

Avant qu'apparussent
Des choses timides

Qui allaient sans toi
Qui t'abandonnaient,

Où poussaient des yeux.

*

S'il est vrai qu'en toi
Commença la vie,

Est-ce une raison
Pour que tu nous tiennes

Comme des complices?

*

Quand les bruyantes charrettes
Cahotaient dans les chemins creux

Où de la vieille boue
Était à demeure, témoignant
Pour les eaux vaincues, acceptant,

Before us
You were there,

Before the timid
things appeared

Who got along without you
Who abandoned you,

There where eyes sprouted.

*

If it is true that in you
Life began,

Is that any reason
You should keep us

As accomplices?

*

When the rattling wagons
Jolted in the sunken lanes

Where old mud
Had settled, bearing witness
To the vanquished waters, accepting,

Tu te tendais à travers l'air
Au long du jour,

Toi sans lèvres,
Pour un baiser.

*

Parfois sur une lande
Où l'on te voyait de loin,

C'était une fête
De la lumière et du vent léger,
Toute couleur presque évanouie.

L'étendue
Ne guettait plus de proie.

L'horizontal s'acceptait,
Durer devenait possible.

*

Encore une fois,
Que faire avec toi,
Nous qui pouvons?

Debout au soleil,
Fiers de nos travaux,
Toujours approchant d'un plus grand secret

Et toi un remords
À n'en pas finir.

*

You spread out along the air
The live-long day,

Lipless one,
For a kiss.

*

Sometimes on a dune
Watching you from afar,

It was a feast
Of light and light wind,
All colour nearly evaporated.

And the sky
No longer sought any prey.

The horizontal was itself,
To abide became possible.

*

Once again,
What to do with you,
We who can?

Upright in the sun,
Proud of our feats,
Always approaching a greater secret

And you a remorse
Never finished.

*

Et du noir,
Rien que du noir
Ou à peu pres,

À cette frange près pour la lumière,
Tellement peu.

J'arrive mal
À y penser.

*

Tu viens et tu vas
Mais dans des limites

Fixées par une loi
Qui n'est pas de toi.

Nous avons en commun
L'expérience du mur.

*

And darkness,
Nothing but darkness
Or nearly,

Except for that fringe for light,
So little.

I find it hard
To think of it.

*

You come and you go
But inside limits

Determined by a law
Which is not yours.

We have in common
The experience of the wall.

*

Venant vers nous de l'horizontal
Tout à fait ouvert,

Venant comme d'une grotte
Aux relents secrets,

Dans ton souffle
Il y a de la préhistoire
Avec du visqueux

Et la gifle en pleine face
D'une jeunesse à emporter
Pour tous les sangs.

*

Rêvant toujours d'aller sur toi
Jusqu'au large où l'on ne voit plus que toi,
Rien de la terre,

Un jour
Je l'ai pu.

Mais je n'ai trouvé que de la surface
Où peut-être j'avançais,

Du volume indéterminé
Où mes cris ne portaient pas.

*

Coming at us from the horizontal
Completely open,

Coming as from a grotto
Of secret musks,

In your breath
There is prehistory
With slimy viscosity

And the slap in full face
Of youth on offer
To fire the blood.

*

Dreaming always of sailing on you
As far as the open sea where one can see only you,
Nothing of land,

One day
I brought it off.

But I found only surface
Where perhaps I advanced,

Of indeterminate volume
Where my cries did not carry.

*

Tous les paysages
Qu'il a fallu voir.

Tous les paysages
Où tu n'étais pas

Et qui t'accusaient
De n'y être pas.

*

Et même si mes heures,
Si chacune d'entre elles,
Comme j'en rêve,

Me valait une année
Que je vis maintenant
Ou me valait un siècle,

Si le coq au matin
Criait pendant un siècle,

Si le soleil mettait
Des siècles à monter,

Est-ce que je pourrais
M'habituer à toi?

*

All the landscapes
One had to see.

All the landscapes
Where you were not

And which accused you
Of not being there.

*

And even if my hours,
If every one of them,
As I dream might be,

Merited me a year
Which I live now
Or merited me a century,

If the cock at dawn
Cried through a century,

If the sun took
Centuries to climb,

Could I ever get
Used to you?

*

Toi, ce creux
Et définitif.

Moi qui rêvais
De faire équilibre.

You, that trough –
Definitive.

I who dreamt
Of finding equilibrium.

Bloodaxe Contemporary French Poets

Series Editors: Timothy Mathews & Michael Worton

FRENCH-ENGLISH BILINGUAL EDITIONS

1: **Yves Bonnefoy:** *On the Motion and Immobility of Douve /
Du mouvement et de l'immobilité de Douve*
Trans. Galway Kinnell. Introduction: Timothy Mathews. £7.95

2: **René Char:** *The Dawn Breakers / Les Matinaux*
Trans. & intr. Michael Worton. [out of print]

3: **Henri Michaux:** *Spaced, Displaced / Déplacements Dégagements*
Trans. David & Helen Constantine. Introduction: Peter Broome.
[out of print]

4: **Aimé Césaire:** *Notebook of a Return to My Native Land /
Cahier d'un retour au pays natal*
Trans. & intr. Mireille Rosello (with Annie Pritchard). £12

5: **Philippe Jaccottet:** *Under Clouded Skies / Beauregard
Pensées sous les nuages / Beauregard*
Trans. David Constantine & Mark Treharne.
Introduction: Mark Treharne. £8.95

6: **Paul Éluard:** *Unbroken Poetry II / Poésie ininterrompue II*
Trans. Gilbert Bowen. Introduction: Jill Lewis. [out of print]

7: **André Frénaud:** *Rome the Sorceress / La Sorcière de Rome*
Trans. Keith Bosley. Introduction: Peter Broome. £8.95

8: **Gérard Macé:** *Wood Asleep / Bois dormant*
Trans. David Kelley. Introduction: Jean-Pierre Richard. £8.95

9: **Guillevic:** *Carnac*
Trans. John Montague. Introduction: Stephen Romer. £12

10: **Salah Stétié:** *Cold Water Shielded: Selected Poems*
Trans. & intr. Michael Bishop. £9.95

'Bloodaxe's Contemporary French Poets series could not have arrived at a more opportune time, and I cannot remember any translation initiative in the past thirty years that has been more ambitious or more coherently planned in its attempt to bring French poetry across the Channel and the Atlantic. Under the editorship of Timothy Mathews and Michael Worton, the series has a clear format and an even clearer sense of mission' – MALCOLM BOWIE, *TLS*

John Montague (1929-2016) was one of Ireland's leading poets, and was the first holder of the Ireland Chair of Poetry. He published three books of poetry with Bloodaxe during the 1980s. His major poetry publications include *The Rough Field*, *The Great Cloak*, *The Dead Kingdom*, *Mount Eagle*, *Time in Armagh* and *Smashing the Piano*. His *Collected Poems* appeared from the Gallery Press in 1995, the year he received the American Ireland Fund Literary Award. His later Gallery titles include *Drunken Sailor* (2004) and *Speech Lessons* (2011). His *New Collected Poems* was published in 2012, and followed by his posthumously published final collection *Second Childhood* in 2017. He translated Francis Ponge's *Selected Poems* with Margaret Guiton and C.K. Williams (Wake Forest University Press, USA & Faber, UK).

Stephen Romer has lived in France since 1981. He is Maître de Conferences at the University of Tours, and has published poetry collections with OUP and Carcanet. He translated Jacques Dupin's *Selected Poems* with Paul Auster and David Shapiro (Wake Forest University Press, USA & Bloodaxe Books, UK). His recent translations include *L'Arrière-Pays* (2012) by Yves Bonnefoy and an anthology, *French Decadent Tales* (2013). He co-edited Bonnefoy's *Poems* (2017) and *Prose* (2020) for Carcanet.